CHRISTIAN'S GUIDE TO GROWING UP

BOYS' & GIRLS' QUESTIONS ANSWERED BY TV'S FAVOURITE DOCTOR

Dr Christian Jessen

Illustrated by
David Semple

SCHOLASTIC

With thanks to Anita Ganeri for her vital help and invaluable input.

Scholastic Children's Books,
Euston House, 24 Eversholt Street,
London NW1 1DB, UK

A division of Scholastic Ltd
London ~ New York ~ Toronto ~ Sydney ~ Auckland
Mexico City ~ New Delhi ~ Hong Kong

Published in the UK by Scholastic Ltd, 2013

Text Copyright © Dr Christian Jessen, 2013
Illustrations © David Semple, 2013
Cover Photography © johnwrightphoto.com

All rights reserved. Moral rights asserted.

ISBN 978 1407 13271 6

Printed and bound by Tien Wah Press Pte. Ltd, Malaysia

8 10 9

CONTENTS

DR CHRISTIAN

HELLO

baby me

Welcome to my extra-special growing up guide just for you! I wrote this to help explain to you all those strange goings on that happen to your body as you get older. Some of the changes may seem a bit embarrassing, so I thought it might be easier for you to read about them here, rather than having to ask your parents or a teacher, although of course you can always do that too.

Your friends will tell you things that may sound scary or a bit unbelievable. Some of them may be true, but a lot will be exaggerated or even completely made up. What you read here is what actually goes on. The truth. So you can put them right about the facts.

How do I know all these things? Well first I am a doctor and so it is my job to know, but also because I have been through all the changes that I write about in this book. Well, all the boys' ones anyway! So I write from experience. It would have been really useful to have a book like this then to help explain what was going on.

The more you know about your body as you grow up the better placed you will be at making sure you are as fit, strong and healthy as you can be. You have some great times ahead of you, so I hope this book will help you to enjoy those times safely, healthily and happily.

Happy reading!

Dr Christian

GIRLS

AN OVERVIEW

Puberty is the time when your body starts changing from a child's body into an adult's. For girls, this usually happens between the ages of nine and 13 but you can be older or younger than that. Everyone is different and develops at different speeds.

Puberty happens because of powerful chemicals, called hormones, which whizz around your body in your bloodstream, sending messages to different parts of your body. Some of these hormones tell your body to grow; others are sex hormones. The result is lots of big changes both on the outside and inside of your body.

These changes get your body ready for being an adult and all the things adults do.

Puberty can be exciting, confusing and scary. Apart from physical changes, your emotions and feelings may be on a roller-coaster journey, too. Don't worry – it's all a normal part of growing up – but it can help to be clued-up about what's happening so that you can stay healthy, happy and safe.

EMOTIONAL ROLLERCOASTER

CHANGES ON THE OUTSIDE

The changes that happen on the outside of your body are probably the ones that you'll notice first. All of a sudden, you'll be much more aware of your body and start noticing how your friends' bodies look too. You can find out much more about these changes later on in this book but here's a quick list for a start. Your body doesn't necessarily change in this order, and some of these stages can overlap.

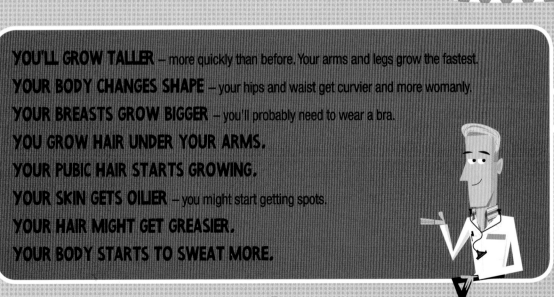

YOU'LL GROW TALLER – more quickly than before. Your arms and legs grow the fastest.

YOUR BODY CHANGES SHAPE – your hips and waist get curvier and more womanly.

YOUR BREASTS GROW BIGGER – you'll probably need to wear a bra.

YOU GROW HAIR UNDER YOUR ARMS.

YOUR PUBIC HAIR STARTS GROWING.

YOUR SKIN GETS OILIER – you might start getting spots.

YOUR HAIR MIGHT GET GREASIER.

YOUR BODY STARTS TO SWEAT MORE.

CHANGES ON THE INSIDE

While changes are happening on the outside,
there are lots of changes happening inside you. Again,
you can find out much more about these changes
later in the book.

- YOUR OVARIES START PRODUCING FEMALE SEX HORMONES.
- YOUR SEX ORGANS GROW AND DEVELOP – YOUR VAGINA STARTS TO CHANGE SHAPE.
- YOU START GETTING VAGINAL DISCHARGE – LIKE A YELLOW OR WHITE STAIN IN YOUR PANTS.
- YOUR PERIODS START.

FEELINGS...

Puberty isn't all about how your body changes physically, though.
It can play havoc with your feelings. You might start to feel incredibly self-
conscious, as if everyone is watching you. You might feel more tired than usual.
Some girls feel emotional and have lots of mood swings, feeling happy one
minute, then like crying the next. This is all quite normal and part of
your body changing from a child's to an adult's. Don't worry,
you will soon get quite used to the new you!

Ask Dr Christian

Meanwhile... What happens to boys?
(from a girl's point of view)

Let's be honest. Boys can be tricky. One minute they seem friendly and grown up, the next they are in a gang driving you crazy and acting like babies! But puberty can be a strange time for boys.

Girls grow very fast, sometimes starting as young as eight, they can get their periods, and they stop growing all in quite a short time. Boys take a bit longer. They may not have a major growth spurt until 15 or 16, and they sometimes keep growing into their early 20s. That's why in class most girls seem so much taller than boys.

Boys who develop slower and are smaller than other boys may feel really stressed about it. On top of that, boys' voices become deeper and may start to crack. If a boy seems pretty shy about talking to you or speaking up in class at this age, it could be that he feels awkward about the way he is growing and changing.

My advice? Don't worry about how they are now, but think about what they will become later.

BOYS >

AN OVERVIEW

Boys usually reach puberty – the time during which a child's body changes into an adult's – between the ages of nine and 15. You may be younger or older than this, as every person is different and each boy develops at his own pace. So don't worry, things will soon settle down.

Your body changes because the tiny pituitary gland at the base of your brain starts producing chemicals called hormones. This kickstarts other glands into releasing more hormones throughout your body. The most important hormone is testosterone – it tells your body to grow and makes changes to your sex organs so that you will able to start a family one day.

All of these changes are very exciting, but puberty can also be pretty tough at times. You may feel all sorts of new and strange emotions as the hormones zoom around your body. It's totally normal, so don't worry about it!

It's good to have an idea of what to expect, so read on to find out all the must-know facts about becoming a man.

YOUR FACIAL BONES GROW, lengthening your face so that you look less boyish and more like a man.

YOU'LL GET TALLER and heavier.

PUBIC HAIR STARTS TO GROW around your genitals.

YOUR VOICE WILL 'BREAK' and get deeper.

YOUR SHOULDERS MAY BECOME BROADER and more muscular.

YOUR SEX ORGANS INCREASE in size.

YOU'LL START TO GROW HAIR in your armpits and on your face.

TALLER

11

CHANGES ON THE INSIDE

It's not just your physical appearance that changes
during puberty – your body changes on the inside as well.
We'll look at these changes in more detail later on, but here's
the lowdown on what's going on behind the scenes.

- YOUR TESTICLES START PRODUCING MALE SEX CELLS CALLED SPERM
- YOUR SKIN GETS OILIER - THIS CAN BLOCK YOUR SKIN PORES AND CAUSES SPOTS.
- YOUR SWEAT GLANDS BECOME MORE ACTIVE, SO THAT YOU START TO PERSPIRE MORE, ESPECIALLY UNDER YOUR ARMS.

FEELINGS...

Becoming a man isn't just about physical changes. All those hormones rushing through
your body can have a big effect on your feelings. Even if you're normally a happy
person, you might feel sad or sensitive at times. You may also have trouble
controlling your temper and get angry about things that never used to bother you.
You could experience sudden mood swings when you're happy one minute and
sad the next. It might feel like you're growing apart from your family and that
no one understands you. This is all totally normal – both your body and
mind are going through a major upheaval! As you move into
adulthood, you'll start to view people and the world around
you from a new, grown-up perspective. It's a big
change, but all boys go through it –
so don't panic!

Ask Dr Christian

Right. What happens to girls?
(from a boy's perspective)

Girls can seem rather older and intimidating, even if they are the same age and in the same class as you. They may make you feel a bit immature and can seem distant. There are reasons for this. Girls tend to go through puberty more quickly than us boys and it can be all over and done for them before it has even started for us. This can make them feel a bit older and more superior to boys, and they can show it. But don't worry, boys soon catch up within a year or two and things even out. Girls may seem more interested in older boys than those in your class, but again this will soon even out.

GIRLS

ON THE OUTSIDE

SHAPING UP

One of the first things you'll notice as you hit puberty is that your body changes shape. You'll get taller more quickly than ever before. This is called a growth spurt. You'll probably grow fastest between the ages of 12 and 13 and carry on growing for around two to three years. At first, your arms and legs grow faster than the rest of your body. This can feel pretty strange but the rest of you will soon catch up. It's quite normal to feel a bit clumsy and out of sorts with yourself while you're growing and getting used to your new shape.

FACT FLASH
While you're growing, you might notice some strange aches and pains. They're sometimes called 'growing pains'. They'll usually go away on their own and don't need any special treatment.

Your body will also start filling out. Your hips get wider and curvier, and you'll probably put on some weight. How curvy you eventually get also depends on your natural body shape. Everyone's different — just look at your friends. These changes are completely normal, and nothing to worry about. It definitely doesn't mean that you're getting fat. They're all part of getting your body ready for having babies one day.

Ask Dr Christian

Why do girls grow faster?

Most girls experience fast growth early in puberty, while boys start growing a bit later. That's why many girls are taller than boys in some classes. You may feel a little bit clumsy and gangly, or not very elegant, and this is probably because your arms and legs grow first, before your trunk. Most girls grow fastest in the 6 months before they have their first period.

Girls also tend to have more fat than boys. You can go from 8% to 21% body fat and this is quite normal, in fact it is healthy. Girl's breasts and hips get bigger and hormones that are being released at this time drive these changes. You may notice more body fat along your upper arms, thighs, and upper back. Your hips will grow rounder and wider; your waist will become narrower. Do not try to slow down your weight gain by changing your diet as this can seriously affect your health. If you are worried about your weight in any way then go and have a chat with a parent, a teacher or your doctor.

HAIR EVERYWHERE

Puberty is also the time when your body gets hairier. You start to grow hair in places that you've never had hair before. Again, it's nothing to worry about. Usually, the first hair to grow is your pubic hair. It's short, curly and wiry, and grows in a triangle shape in your groin. About a year later, you'll also find that hair starts growing in your armpits. You might get a few dark hairs around your nipples, and the hairs on your arms, legs and upper lip may get darker in colour.

GETTING RID OF HAIR

Everyone has hair on their bodies and it's fine just to leave it alone. But while boys might be busy boasting about it, some girls don't like it, especially if they've got dark hair and it's more noticeable. It's a very personal thing. If it doesn't bother you, you can leave it to grow naturally. But if you're not happy here are some of the ways you can remove it:

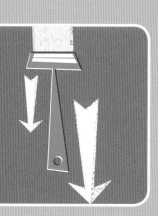

SHAVING

Pros: Quick; easy; cheap
Cons: Scratches; razor-burn; stubbly regrowth
Tips: Never dry shave. Use a clean razor and shaving foam for sensitive skin. Pat with a cool flannel afterwards.

HAIR-REMOVAL CREAM

Pros: Softer regrowth; pain-free
Cons: Messy; can irritate the skin; smells terrible
Tips: Follow the instructions carefully. Test the cream on a small patch of skin first.

WAXING

Pros: Works well; hair grows back slowly
Cons: Painful, like ripping off a sticking plaster
Tips: For best results, get it done in a salon. If using a waxing kit at home, practise on your legs first.

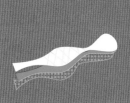

PLUCKING

Pros: Cheap; easy; convenient
Cons: Time-consuming; no good for large areas of hair
Tips: Use a good pair of tweezers; don't prod or gouge your skin too much.

ELECTROLYSIS

Pros: Permanent
Cons: Very expensive; can be painful
Tips: ONLY get this done at a proper salon that's been recommended.

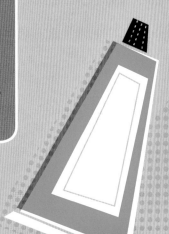

GROWING BREASTS

A clear sign that your body's
changing is when you start growing
breasts. Some girls are thrilled when this
happens and can't wait to wear a bra. Other girls
can feel self-conscious and think that people are staring
at them. But what are breasts for? They're mainly for feeding
any babies that you might have with nourishing breast milk.
Many people think that they're also attractive to look at, and
they're sensitive to being touched.

11 12 13 14 15 16 17 18 19 20 21

Breasts grow slowly. First, the circle of skin (called the areola) around your nipple
swells and gets darker. Then a small bump, called a breast 'bud', grows
underneath. Your breasts start to fill out (they're mostly made of fat
which protects the milk-making parts inside), and your nipples get
bigger and darker. Don't worry if your breasts are cone-shaped
for a while. They'll round out after a year or so. And don't
worry if your breasts feel tender or tingly while
they're growing. That's completely
normal, too.

Getting a bra

When you feel your breasts wobbling as you walk, it may be time to get a bra. You don't have to wear a bra at all but, if your breasts are quite large and heavy, a bra can help support them and make you feel more comfortable, especially if you're doing exercise.

The right bra

Getting the right fit can be tricky. Your bra should fit snugly around your ribs so that it's comfortable but doesn't ride up at the back. The cups should hold your breasts firmly but shouldn't be so big that they sag or so small that you bulge out at the sides. If you're still not sure about which bra to buy, it's a good idea to go for a proper bra fitting. Some large stores offer a free measuring service. You'll be measured in a changing room and you'll probably be asked to take off your top. It can be a bit scary, especially the first time, so you might want to take your mum or a friend along, but it's worth it to get a bra that really fits.

23 24 25 26 27 28 29 30 31 32

Don't forget, though, that your body will carry on growing and developing over the next few years so you'll need to have regular measurings to check that your bra still fits.

Types of bra

Try on some different bras to find one that you like and fits well. There are all sorts of bras to choose from. Put your top on over each bra so you see if it gives you a good shape.

FIRST BRAS

Comfortable, with soft cups; give you a natural shape.

MULTIWAY BRAS

Straps can be altered for wearing under different tops.

CROP TOPS

No cups but gives support; better for smaller breasts.

SPORTS BRAS

Keeps your breasts in place while you exercise.

FACT FLASH

Some bras are underwired which means that they have wires in the cups to hold larger breasts up. These aren't recommended for younger girls whose breasts are still developing.

Ask Dr Christian

Am I normal? – girls' breasts

Girls can worry that their breasts haven't developed quite like their friends'. It can be the change that stresses them out the most. For girls the changes of puberty can all happen very quickly. Along with growing curvier hips, your breasts grow and a network of milk ducts develops inside them. But your breasts can continue to grow until you're 17 or 18 years old and even older, and it is quite normal for one breast to grow faster than the other, although the slower one usually catches up. Some girls worry about the colour and shape of their nipples. They can become pink or dark brown, or turn inward or out. All of this is normal too. If you want to get an idea about what your breasts might look like as a woman, look at your mum. Your final breast size is based partly on your family. Your breasts won't be exactly like your mum's because your father's genes also play a part, but they can give you a rough idea. Oh and by the way, it is NOT true that squeezing your breast buds will stimulate them to grow bigger. You may actually end up damaging them, so don't try it.

BOYS

ON THE OUTSIDE

SHAPING UP

Boys get taller and heavier during puberty. Your shoulders and chest broaden and your upper body gets more muscular. As the upper body gets wider, the hips may appear narrower in comparison – a man's torso can look a bit like an upside-down triangle! You'll grow quickly over about three to four years – this is called a growth spurt. You won't grow at the same pace all over, though. Your feet and hands get bigger, then your arms and legs get longer. You might feel awkward with long limbs, and super-sized hands or feet, but the rest of your body will catch up later on!

FACT FLASH
As you develop, you'll find your body shape will probably fall into one of three main body types – ectomorph (tall and thin), endomorph (rounder body, shorter arms and legs) and mesomorph (muscular, broad shoulders, narrow waist, long limbs).

Movie stars, sportsmen and male models often appear to have the ideal male body shape – tall, lean and muscular. This combination of mesomorph and ectomorph body types (see Fact Flash) is quite unusual. Staying fit, eating healthily, regular exercise and a positive attitude are way better than worrying you don't have a 'perfect' body. Be happy with the way you look – you're unique!

Ask Dr Christian

Am I normal? - Slow developers - boys

It can be rough starting puberty later than your friends. You may have noticed them growing bigger and taller, and their voices changing, but not much seems to be happening with you. It's not uncommon to feel shorter than everybody else, or for people to think you are younger than you are. You may even get a bit left behind playing sports or in PE.

But don't worry. Your body will catch up. There is very rarely anything wrong with boys who start puberty later. Actually, it probably runs in your family. Ask your parents if they remember when it happened to them, and the chances are, they will have started growing later too.

It may even be that you are right on track and in line with everyone else, but just haven't noticed it yet. Boys go through puberty between the ages of about nine to 14, with the average age being around 12. We would only think it late if nothing were happening by around 14.

HAIRY SITUATION

Growing body hair is a big part of becoming a man. During puberty, short, curly pubic hairs start to appear around your genitals and between your legs. The hairs on your legs and arms grow longer and may thicken and darken. Hair sprouts from your armpits, and it may also grow on your chest, abdomen, back and feet. Towards the end of puberty, facial hair begins to grow on your upper lip, cheeks and chin.

SHAVING

Boys are usually aged between 14 and 16 when their first facial hairs appear. Lightly coloured hairs grow above the upper lip, becoming darker and thicker over time. Hair also starts to grow on the cheeks, chin and upper neck.

Some boys are able to grow a full beard by the time they're 18. For others, it may take until their mid-20s until they have some serious stubble! And some men never grow more than a few whiskers – at least they save money on razor blades!

FACT FLASH
Don't use ordinary soap instead of shaving foam or gel as this hardens the stubble and dulls the sharpness of your razor blade.

24

HOW TO SHAVE →

First, decide if you want to shave with a razor or an electric shaver. A razor cuts closer than an electric shaver, but you can get nicks and cuts if you're not careful! It's best to use a quality multi-blade cartridge razor. This costs more than a cheap, disposable razor but gives you a smoother shave that's less likely to irritate your skin and give you 'razor rash'.

1. USE WARM WATER TO WET YOUR FACE. Soften your stubble and lubricate the skin using shaving cream or gel – never shave a dry face as this will make your skin very sore and increase the risk of cuts and nicks.

2. PULL THE SKIN OF YOUR FACE TAUT and shave in the direction of the hair growth. Rinse your blade with warm water regularly to get rid of the cut hairs.

3. YOU MAY WANT TO SHAVE UPWARDS – against the direction of hair growth – on your neck and under your chin for a closer shave, but be careful as it's easier to nick yourself doing this.

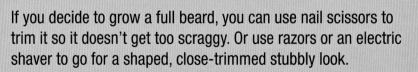

If you decide to grow a full beard, you can use nail scissors to trim it so it doesn't get too scraggy. Or use razors or an electric shaver to go for a shaped, close-trimmed stubbly look.

SWEATING IT OUT

Your skin is covered in sweat glands that release sweat onto your skin when you're hot. The heat from your body evaporates the sweat, which helps to cool you down. When you're a child this isn't a problem, but when you hit puberty it can lead to stinky, smelly BO – Body Odour. The sweat glands in your armpits become active and the bacteria on your skin multiply in the moist, warm conditions. This creates the nasty whiff of BO. You can help reduce this by taking a bath or shower every day, especially after exercise when you've been sweating a lot, and using a deodorant or antiperspirant.

Ask Dr Christian

Help! I think I might be growing breasts!

Some boys may notice their nipples and chest area becoming a little sore, and can even start to stick out and look a bit like a girl's. This isn't a medical problem and it doesn't mean you will grow breasts. I know because when I was growing up I had the same problem, and I didn't grow boobs, so neither will you! It is actually quite a normal thing to happen during puberty, even if it does seem a little embarrassing, and about half of all boys going through puberty will experience it so you are definitely not alone. It occurs because of an imbalance in the hormones testosterone and oestrogen, which go up and down a lot as you are growing and are responsible for all the changes that you will notice. These hormones will settle down in time however. This means that the tender lumps you can feel behind your nipples should go away after a while.

Ask Dr Christian

What is a foreskin?

A foreskin is the sleeve of skin that covers the end of your penis. It protects the sensitive head of your penis and has many different functions. Normally you will be able to pull your foreskin back so that you can wash all around your penis – this can make peeing easier and a lot less messy. Some boys may have a foreskin that is a bit too tight and can't be easily pulled back. It can be difficult to clean and may hurt when you get an erection. If you think you might have this problem then you should tell your parents or your doctor who can talk about various ways to help you. Sometimes it can get a bit smelly under there and you may see some white stuff around the head of your penis. This builds up naturally during the day, particularly when it is hot or you have been running around exercising. Make sure that you wash it carefully every time you take a bath or shower, by gently pulling your foreskin right back.

My friend has been circumcised — why?

All boys are born with a foreskin. Some boys have an operation called a circumcision to remove this skin. It is mainly done for religious reasons but is not medically necessary. The foreskin has useful functions and would only be removed medically if it was too tight and causing pain or other problems.

There is no difference in hygiene or function between a circumcised or uncircumcised willy.

SKIN DEEP

Spots, zits, pimples, acne, call them what you like. Lots of people get them and it doesn't matter if you're a boy or a girl. As if you haven't got enough to worry about, suddenly your skin breaks out in a load of lumps and bumps. So what are spots? Why do you get them? And what can you do to get rid of them?

Your skin produces a kind of oil, called sebum. It's made in the sebaceous glands under your skin. Sebum is really useful – it helps to protect your skin and keep it supple and waterproof. But, during puberty, your hormones send sebum-production into overdrive. The extra oil can clog up the glands, causing spots and pimples on your skin.

Some spots are tiny and painless but bacteria that live on the sebum can cause them to become red, angry and inflamed.

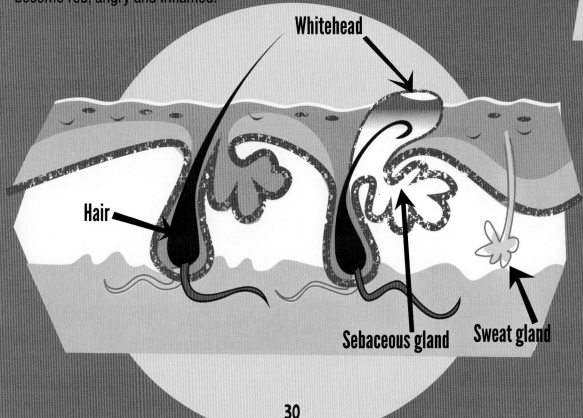

Whitehead

Hair

Sebaceous gland

Sweat gland

ACNE TRUE OR FALSE?

Acne is caused by not cleansing your skin. False! Acne is caused by excess oil, dead skin cells, and bacteria becoming trapped within a hair follicle, causing a spot.

Eating chocolate causes acne. False! There is no link between chocolate and acne, although eating too much chocolate can make you gain weight, leading to other problems.

Greasy fried foods cause acne. False! In fact there is no proven link between diet and acne. Bacteria have a greater impact on breakouts than your diet.

Blackheads are caused by dirt trapped in the pore. False! The black top of a blackhead is not dirt. It's an accumulation of dead skin cells and sebum that changes to a dark brown or black colour when exposed to air.

You can catch acne from someone else. False! Acne is not contagious. You can't catch it by shaking hands, touching, or even kissing someone with acne.

You should vigorously scrub your skin every day to help stop spots growing. False! People with acne have a tendency to really scrub their face, trying to deeply cleanse the pores to get that 'squeaky-clean' feeling, but this can make things worse, not better.

There is nothing you can do about acne. False! Today there are loads of treatments available to improve acne. Acne is not something you must suffer through. Nearly every case of acne can be successfully controlled with time, persistence, and patience.

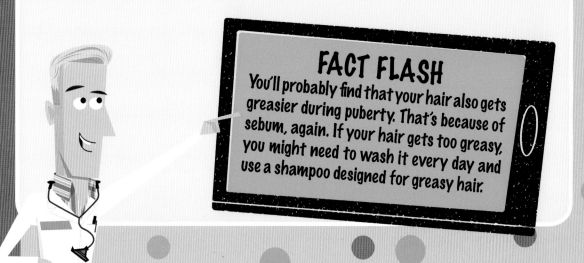

FACT FLASH

You'll probably find that your hair also gets greasier during puberty. That's because of sebum, again. If your hair gets too greasy, you might need to wash it every day and use a shampoo designed for greasy hair.

COPING WITH SPOTS

The good news is that spots mostly clear up by themselves after a few days and they usually go for good after puberty. The bad news is that you've got a party to go to and you want to get rid of them now! So what can you do?

There are lots of spot remedies out there and it can be really confusing. It's really a case of finding the one that works best for you. Here are some things you can try at home:

• Keep your skin in good condition by eating a healthy diet and drinking plenty of water. It won't stop you getting spots but it can help.

• Wash your face twice a day with warm water or mild soap, then gently pat it dry. Scrubbing encourages your skin to make more oil.

• Don't be tempted to squeeze or pick at your spots. It'll make them last longer and there's the risk of being left with tiny scars.

• Avoid using make-up or other beauty products. Trying to cover spots up with foundation and concealers just makes things worse.

• Try one of the spot treatments you can buy at the chemist's, like medicated lotions, facewashes and creams. They should clear up mild acne in a few weeks.

Ask Dr Christian

When do spots become acne?

The exact definition of acne doesn't really matter. If you are worried about your spots and you are making you unhappy, then that is a good enough reason to go to your doctor to ask for some help and treatment. There is no need to suffer with it for a long time and doing so may mean you end up with permanent scars where the spots were. Go and get it sorted as there are plenty of treatments available to you on prescription from your GP that can be very effective.

GIRLS >

ON THE INSIDE

The changes happening on the outside of your body are easy to see but there are plenty of changes going on inside you, too. They're caused by your body making female sex hormones (mainly oestrogen and progesterone), preparing your body for having babies one day. For this, big changes need to happen to your sex organs which are mostly tucked away inside your tummy, protected by your pelvic bones.

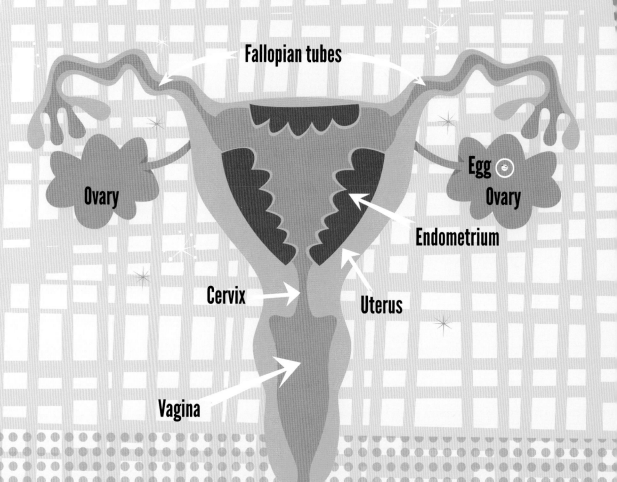

Fallopian tubes

Ovary

Egg

Ovary

Endometrium

Cervix

Uterus

Vagina

Fallopian tubes:

These narrow tubes run from your ovaries to your uterus. Eggs from your ovaries travel along the tubes.

Ovaries:

You have two ovaries, one on each side of your body. They are where the eggs (ova) needed to make babies are stored. Each ovary is about the size and shape of a walnut, and contains hundreds of thousands of eggs.

Endometrium:

The inner lining of your uterus that contains many blood vessels that help a fertilized egg to attach itself and grow into a baby.

Cervix:

This is the neck or entrance to your uterus. It connects the uterus to the vagina.

Uterus (womb):

Your uterus is where a baby grows if you are pregnant. It is usually about the size and shape of an upside-down pear but it stretches as the baby gets bigger.

Vagina:

A stretchy tube of muscle that leads from your uterus to the outside of your body. It lets blood out during your period, and holds tampons in place. A man's penis fits inside it during sex. Babies travel down it to be born.

Vulva:

Your vulva is the name for the sex organs on the outside of your body. It's mostly covered by your pubic hair. It's protected by several folds of skin, called the labia. These get larger during puberty. Between the labia, there's a tiny bump, called the clitoris, which is very sensitive to touch. Just like boys, some girls like to masturbate by gently stroking the area around their clitoris. Sometimes this can create an exciting throbbing sensation known as an orgasm. Below the clitoris is the opening to your vagina.

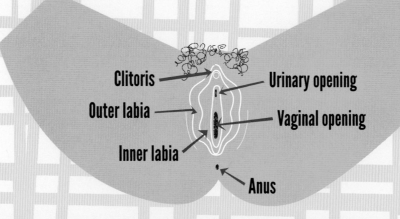

Clitoris — Urinary opening

Outer labia — Vaginal opening

Inner labia

Anus

STARTING YOUR PERIODS

Having your first period is a really big deal but it's not as scary as it sounds. It's a normal sign that your body is healthy and growing up and is nothing to worry or feel embarrassed about. So, what are periods? How do they happen? And when do they start?

Periods happen when your body is developed enough to have babies. Each month, your ovaries release a ripe egg which travels down your fallopian tube towards your uterus. At the same time, a thick lining grows in your uterus so that a baby can grow there. If the egg doesn't meet a sperm, and isn't fertilised, it doesn't grow into a baby and breaks down. The thick lining of the uterus isn't needed either,

and it also breaks down. It comes out of your vagina as blood – your period has started.

The time from the start of one period to another is called the menstrual cycle. It usually lasts for about 28 days, though it can be longer or shorter than that. When your periods first start, they might not be regular for a while but they'll soon settle down.

28 days

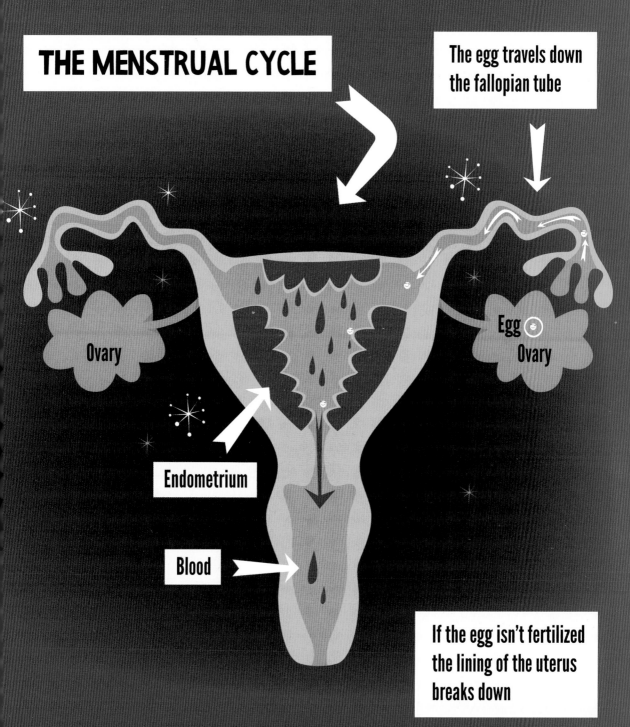

COPING WITH PERIODS

There's no reason that life shouldn't go on as usual while you're having your period. You can still do everything you normally do. You just need to make sure that you're wearing the right sanitary products. You can choose sanitary towels or tampons – it's up to you and what you feel most comfortable with.

Using towels

Many girls start off using sanitary towels. These are strips of padded material that stick inside your pants and soak up the blood as it comes out. You can buy them in different sizes and thicknesses, depending on how heavy or light your period is. You might need a thicker towel at night, and at the beginning of your period; at other times, you may use a thinner towel.

Sanitary towels are hygienic to use but you should change them regularly, every few hours, even if you don't bleed too much. This stops harmful bacteria collecting and possibly causing a smell or infection. Never flush towels down the toilet. Wrap them up carefully and throw them away in a bin (public and school toilets will have special bins for this).

Using tampons

Tampons are little rolls of absorbent material with a piece of string attached to one end. You put a tampon inside your vagina where it swells up and soaks up blood. Some have a tear-off plastic wrapping – you push them in with your finger. Others come inside a cardboard or plastic tube, called an applicator, which helps to push them up in. Once your tampon's in place, you shouldn't be able to feel it and it shouldn't hurt. The piece of string hangs outside your body so that you can pull the tampon out easily.

As with towels, tampons come in different sizes, depending on how heavy or light your period is. It's best to use the smallest tampon possible but you might need to use different sizes at different times. Change your tampon regularly, especially if your flow is heavy. Otherwise, harmful bacteria may grow on the tampon and there is a risk of Toxic Shock Syndrome, a rare but serious illness. You can usually flush tampons down the toilet or wrap them and put them in a bin, as with towels.

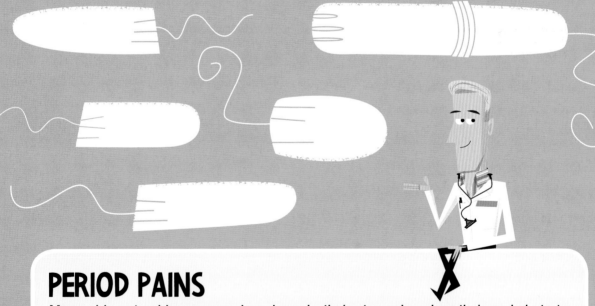

PERIOD PAINS

Many girls get aching cramps low down in their stomachs when their period starts. These are called 'period pains'. You might also get some backache. Doing some exercise, using a hot pad like a hot water bottle, or taking a anti-inflammatory drug like ibuprofen can help. Avoid taking aspirin however. Some girls also get mood swings, feel bloated and have sore breasts. This is called premenstrual syndrome (PMS). Again, exercise and a healthy diet can help to relieve your symptoms.

Ask Dr Christian

Am I Normal? - Periods

I'm 13 and I've not started my periods yet. All my friends started ages ago.

A big marker by which some girls measure their maturity is whether their periods have started. This is of course nonsense because a first period can start any time between ages 11 and 14. But it can be as early as eight or as late as 15. So I would be patient and things should start happening soon enough.

What is important to know is that if your periods have started then you can get pregnant. You can even get pregnant in the month before your first period starts.

Why do I get so grumpy before my period?

You may notice that being on or near your period makes you feel a bit tense or emotional. You may even feel a bit bloated, your breasts may be tender, and you can sometimes get a few spots on your face. These are all due to the hormone changes that occur in your body during your monthly cycle and although they can be annoying, are quite normal.

My periods started, then stopped again. What's wrong with me?

For the first year or two, your cycle may not be regular and you may not have a period sometimes. If you are underweight because of dieting or exercise, have a lot of stress in your life, or are overweight, your periods may be hard to predict and be irregular.

THE DANGLY BITS (OR ABOUT A BOY'S BITS)

Your body goes through a growth spurt during puberty – and so does your willy! It takes three to four years for your willy, or penis, to reach its final size. Your scrotum – the wrinkly bag of skin between your legs than contains your balls, or testicles – loosens up so that it hangs lower. Your testicles also grow and start producing sperm – male sex cells. Several million sperm are produced every day, ready to fertilize a female egg, or ova, and make a baby.

INSIDE STORY

Your penis is just one part of a complicated reproductive system! Let's take a look at what's going on inside your body as your sex organs become active during puberty...

TESTICLES – Ball-shaped organs that produce sperm cells and the hormone testosterone.

PENIS – The external male sex organ through which you urinate, and when erect is used to deposit sperm.

URETHRA – A tube from the penis to the bladder that allows wee, or urine, to be passed out of the body.

GLANS – The sensitive head of the penis, with a small, central hole for the urethral opening.

FORESKIN – A fold of skin covering the glans.

SEMINAL VESICLES – These glands create a fluid that gives sperm energy.

PROSTATE GLAND – Produces a fluid that sperm can float in, allowing the sex cells to move.

SPERM DUCT – Sperm travels along these ducts from the epididymis to the penis.

SCROTUM – The sac, or bag, of skin that contains the testicles.

BLADDER – a muscular bag that stores your wee until you're ready to go to the toilet.

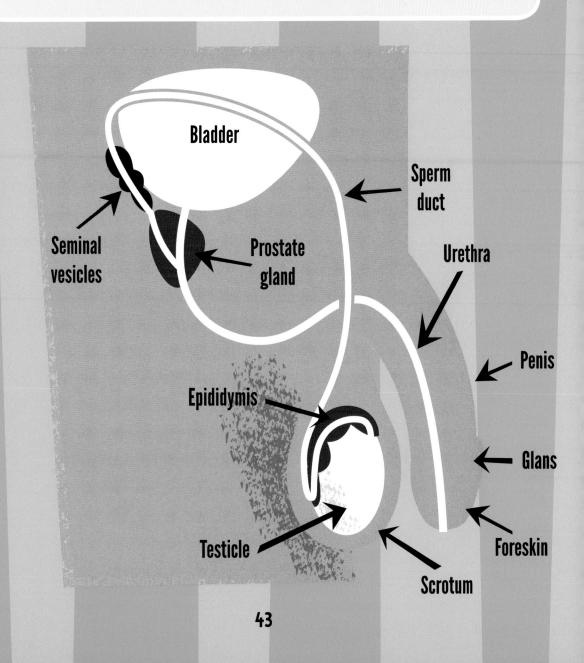

Bladder

Sperm duct

Seminal vesicles

Prostate gland

Urethra

Penis

Epididymis

Glans

Testicle

Scrotum

Foreskin

HARD AND SOFT

A boy's willy is usually soft and floppy, but when you become sexually excited, more blood flows into so it then gets stiff and sticks out from the body. This is called an erection, or 'hard on'. It does this in readiness for having sex.

AN UP AND DOWN ISSUE

Boys start having erections from a very early age. Even babies have them! During puberty, erections become more frequent. They also seem to have a life of their own – your willy can go from soft to hard in seconds! This can be a bit embarrassing – a hard-on can spring up sitting at your desk at school, on a train or bus, or anywhere! You could be thinking about sex, or a vibration could trigger it, or there might be no reason at all.

You may find that you frequently wake up in the morning with an erection. Don't get too stressed about it – it's a stand-up problem every boy goes through!

FACT FLASH

Some erections are curved or point at a slight angle, often to the left – this is very common and nothing to be concerned about.

SIZING IT UP

Some boys become anxious about the size of their willy during puberty. Don't worry! When a smaller penis becomes erect it usually increases in size a lot more than one that is larger in the floppy state – which evens things out. The average length of an erect penis is between 12.5 cm (5 in) and 15.25 cm (6 in).

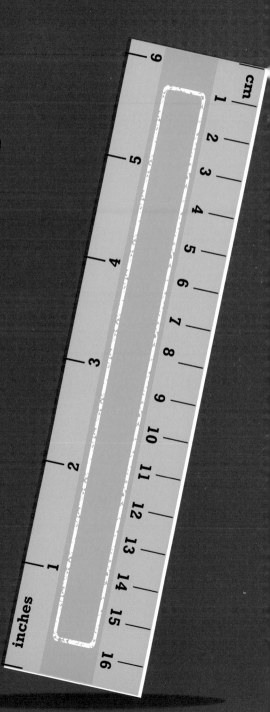

ALL ABOUT EJACULATION

When you are sexually aroused, or 'turned on', sperm mixes with other fluids to create a greyish white fluid called semen. Arousal can build quite quickly to an ejaculation, the process through which the semen is forced out of your willy. It's also called an orgasm, or 'cumming'. When this happens, intense, pleasurable muscle contractions force the semen up through the urethra and out of the opening at the tip of your penis.

WET DREAMS

Sometimes you may ejaculate in your sleep. Don't worry about it. The can happen if you have a sexual dream – you may wake up when you orgasm, or you may not know about it till the next morning! Either way, it's perfectly normal and nothing to be embarrassed about. Just wipe off any stains on your sheets or nightclothes with a paper towel or wet flannel, or put them all in the washing machine.

DOING IT YOURSELF

Giving yourself sexual pleasure, or masturbating, is probably the number one hobby for boys going through puberty! By rubbing your willy up and down with your hand, you can bring yourself to orgasm and ejaculate. This is also called 'wanking'.

There are many myths that masturbation is bad for you but they aren't true – it certainly won't make you go blind! It's healthy, normal and pleasurable – just don't overdo it or you might make your penis rather sore!

FACT FLASH
When you ejaculate, a valve shuts off the bladder so you can't release semen and wee at the same time.

Ask Dr Christian

One of my balls doesn't feel quite right. It has a
sort of lump on it. What should I do?

If you notice anything different about your balls
then you should always tell your parents or a doctor.
This is because there are some problems that can
happen down there that need to be treated as quickly
as possible.

Lumps in the testicles could be many things. Some are
perfectly normal. For example, you may be feeling the
epididymis, the tightly coiled tube where sperm are
stored. Other lumps may be signs of a problem that won't
go away on its own, and need some medical treatment.

It is a good idea to get to know exactly how your body
feels, all over, including your private bits, so that
you will then notice any changes that may occur. Some
changes are a normal part of growing up, but others may
not be quite so normal, and will need to be checked out
by your doctor.

ELSEWHERE IN A BOY'S BODY...

HIGH AND LOW

Your voice box, or larynx, grows during puberty and as it gets bigger, your voice gets deeper. The strip-like muscles, or vocal cords, in your larynx may be a bit unstable as they grow, and sometimes you can momentarily lose control of your voice. This 'wobble' means you can suddenly go from speaking in a deep voice to squeaking like a mouse! It's a bit embarrassing, but your voice will settle down over time.

Your enlarging larynx will also cause a bump to appear in the front of your throat under your chin. This is called your Adam's apple and is another sign that you are growing up.

GROWING PAINS

Boys sometimes get growing pains in their thighs, calves, ankles and knees. Your developing muscles get overtired from too much exercise or activity. This often happens between the ages of eight and 12 and can continue through puberty. Stretching your limbs can help, and you could apply a heating pad or hot-water bottle. You could also take a painkiller, such as ibuprofen or paracetamol.

BULKING UP

Boys become more muscular during puberty. Your heart and lungs also grow larger, giving you greater strength and endurance. This is sometimes called a strength spurt. The upper body grows the most, as the chest and shoulder muscles broaden.

It's important to be patient, though as not everybody naturally develops a superhero physique and a flat, 'six-pack' stomach! You can build up muscle strength from any kind of physical activity, such as running, swimming, cycling or playing football.

ABOUT SEX

For both boys and girls, all the changes you go through at puberty are designed to get your body ready for having babies one day. This can be a long time off but it's useful to know how it happens so that you can be ready and safe. To make a baby, a sperm from a man has to join with an egg inside a woman's body. For this to happen naturally, a man and woman have to have sexual intercourse, also called sex or making love.

During sex, a couple kiss and cuddle. The man's penis becomes hard and stiff so that it can fit inside a woman's vagina. Her vagina releases slippery fluid which makes it easier for the penis to enter. The man pushes his penis inside the vagina where it squirts out a liquid, called semen, which contains millions of sperm. These swim up into the woman's body where one of them might meet an egg, and fertilize it.

But sex isn't just about having babies. It's also a way of getting close to a person and of showing love and affection. Men can have sex with each other, and so can women. It can make people feel very good. But it can also make people feel bad if they have sex when they're not ready or if they do it with someone that they don't trust or like.

Ask Dr Christian

How do I know when I'm ready to have sex?

Having sex is a big step for when you're older. In fact, in the UK, it is against the law to have sex if you're under the age of 16. Even then, you should never have sex because you feel that you have to, or because your friends all seem to be doing it. If you're not ready, don't do it. You don't have to do anything that you don't want to do, and you always have the right to say no. Don't let anyone force you to do anything you feel uncomfortable with.

HOW PREGNANCY WORKS

If a sperm fertilizes an egg, during sex, a baby can begin growing inside a woman's body – the woman is pregnant. As it travels down the fallopian tube, the fertilized egg starts dividing and growing. It then fixes itself safely to the lining of the uterus, where it divides and grows lots more, as it turns into a baby.

As the fertilized egg divides, it forms a tiny embryo. After a while, the embryo starts to look more human, with a head, arms, legs, eyes, nose and ears. From now on, it grows and develops quickly until it is ready to be born at about nine months.

At first, a woman may feel tired, bloated and have sore breasts. She may also feel sick. These are all signs of pregnancy, though not all women experience them all. After the first two months, her tummy starts to grow bigger and her breasts swell, ready to make milk for when the baby is born. When the baby is ready to be born, it usually turns upside down, so that its head pushes out of the vagina first. Giving birth to a baby is called labour.

Ask Dr Christian

Sex mythbusting

You can get pregnant at ANY time of the month. The timing of your cycle is different for everyone, especially for those whose periods that don't start at the same time every month.

Don't rely on your friends' advice about how and when you can get pregnant.

Just to be absolutely clear:
- You CAN get pregnant if you have sex standing up.
- You CAN get pregnant if it's your first time having sex.
- You CAN get pregnant if you do star jumps after sex.
- If a boy doesn't ejaculate inside the vagina, you can still get pregnant.
- If you don't have an orgasm, you CAN still get pregnant.
- Having sex in water DOES NOT prevents you from getting pregnant.
- Douching or washing your vagina out after sex will NOT prevent you from getting pregnant.

CONTRACEPTION

If a couple is ready to have sex but doesn't want to have a baby, they can use contraception to stop the woman getting pregnant or catching infections. There are lots of different forms of contraception. Here are some of the options:

Condoms

A condom is a thin, stretchy sheath that is rolled on to a man's penis before sex. It stops sperm from travelling into the woman's vagina. Condoms are safe and easy to use, and you can buy them from places like the chemist's and supermarket[1].

The Pill

The Pill is a tablet that a woman takes to stop her getting pregnant. Some types of the Pill contain hormones that stop the ovaries releasing eggs. Others contain hormones that make the uterus lining too slippery for eggs to stick to it. Some women also take the Pill to make their periods lighter.

1. They are also the best way of preventing sexually transmitted infections (STIs).

CONDOMS

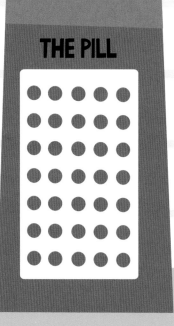

THE PILL

DIAPHRAGM

Diaphragms

Diaphragms are round, rubbery objects that are pushed up inside the vagina. They fit over the cervix (neck of the uterus), blocking sperm. They have to be used with spermicidal cream or gel, and inserted every time a woman has sex.

IUDs

An IUD (Intra-Uterine Device), IUS, or coil, is a tiny plastic and copper object that's fitted inside the uterus by a doctor or nurse. It lasts for five years and stops fertilised eggs from sticking to the lining of the uterus. Some have a tiny bit of hormone added to them.

Injections and implants

These release hormones and work in a similar way to the Pill. An injection can protect a woman for 8-12 weeks. An implant is a tiny tube placed under the skin in a woman's arm and can last for about three years.

All these are available from your doctor or health clinic.

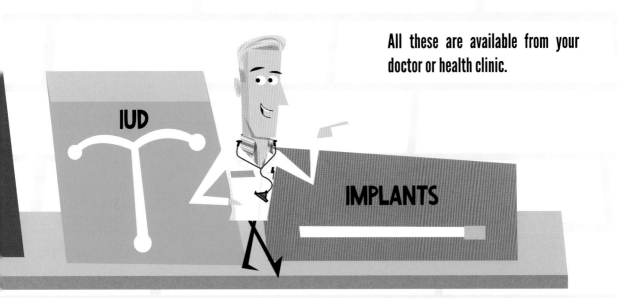

IUD

IMPLANTS

STI GUIDE

Sex should be good. It can be about love, or about friendship. It can be between a man and woman, a man and a man, or a woman and a woman. It can be about making a baby or just about having fun. But it needs to be thought about and care taken or things can go wrong. A pregnancy that is not intended can be a big headache. And sometimes certain diseases, called sexually transmitted infections (or STIs for short), can be passed on by having sex with someone who has an infection. Some are easily treated, others are not.

If you've ever had sex, you may be at risk of having an STI. Your risk is higher if you have had many sex partners, have had sex with someone who has had many partners or have had sex without using condoms. Here are some of the common STIs:

Chlamydia is a bacteria that you can catch through sexual contact with someone who is infected. It is one of the most common STIs in the UK. You may not know that you have it as you can't always feel it but a doctor can do a test for it and it's easily treated with antibiotics.

Human papillomavirus (HPV) is a very common infection. There are many types of HPV. Some types cause genital warts, while other types don't cause any symptoms. Some are connected with cancer of the cervix. Currently, there is no cure for HPV but in many people HPV will eventually go away on its own without causing any health problems. There is a vaccine that you will be offered at school. The vaccine targets the types of HPV that cause up to 70% of all cases of cervical cancer and about 90% of all cases of genital warts. I recommend that you have it!

Human immunodeficiency virus (HIV) attacks the body's immune system making you more likely to get sick from bacteria and viruses. It is also harder for your body to fight off these infections when you do get them, so you may have trouble getting better. HIV is the condition that leads to acquired immunodeficiency syndrome (AIDS). There is no cure but it can be well managed with medicines.

All STIs can be diagnosed by your doctor by having a sexual health screen.

The only sure way to prevent STIs is by not having sex. If you have sex, you can lower your risk of getting an STI by only having sex with someone who isn't having sex with anyone else and who doesn't have an STI. You should always use condoms when having sex, and get tested for these different infections regularly.

MOODS AND FEELINGS

Puberty is not only a time of physical changes. You are changing emotionally, too, and this can be difficult. You find yourself falling out with friends and family, especially your parents, and it might feel as if your emotions are taking over your life. You might feel that no one understands you which can be frustrating and irritating. The trouble is that you're changing from a child into an adult, and this can be a time of life that's filled with great uncertainty and confusion. Your changing feelings are all part of the process of seeing yourself, and other people, in a different way. They might be a pain at the time but something we all go through and will eventually settle down. I know, cos I went through it too!

MOOD SWINGS

During puberty, it's normal to find that your feelings change from one day to the next. You might wake up, feeling on top of the world, but, by the evening, feel angry and sad. Your moods swing from happiness and contentment to anger and irritation so fast that it's difficult to keep up. Mood swings can cause you to be snappy or angry – you might fly into a temper over the tiniest thing. This can make you difficult to live with and cause friction with your family. You might also resent the way your parents still treat you as a child when you think that you're an adult, and this can lead to rows.

58

FEELING SELF-CONSCIOUS

You might start to feel self-conscious, as if the whole world is watching everything you do. You feel shy meeting new people or at parties, and get embarrassed really easily. You want people to notice you but that's also the last thing you want! Feeling self-conscious or shy is very common, especially at a time when your physical appearance is changing so fast and you're having to get used to a whole new you. Lots of people feel just like you do, even if they look calm and confident on the outside.

CRUSHES

Having a crush on someone can be brilliant, overwhelming, heartbreaking or all three at once. It means that you have very strong feelings for someone. This might be someone you know, like a friend, an older adult you know, or even a teacher at your school. It might be someone you don't know, and have no hope of ever meeting, like a famous pop star, footballer or celebrity. You can't choose the person you have a crush on – it just happens. Before you know it, you've fallen head over heels in love with them and can't stop thinking about them. You spend hours daydreaming about them and what it would be like to be with them. You write their name endlessly – your whole world revolves around them. The trouble is that, usually, the object of your crush doesn't feel the same way about you, even if they know who you are. This is called unrequited love and it can feel like the end of the world. You feel as if your heart has been broken and wonder what is wrong with you. These can be very real and painful emotions, and can take a while to get over, though they do eventually fade. Never try to force your feelings on someone, no matter how badly you want them to like you back. The good news is that most crushes only last for a few days or weeks, or a few months at most, so you can soon get your life back on track.

FANCY THAT – FIRST RELATIONSHIPS

During puberty, you might start having feelings for other people that you've never experienced before. You suddenly find yourself attracted to a boy or girl, and begin thinking of them as more than just a friend. Typically, you might feel flustered when you see them and get butterflies in your stomach. You hope that they'll notice you, then wish that the ground would swallow you up if they do. These feelings are caused by your hormones kicking in. They can be very strong, exciting and confusing, but they're also a perfectly normal part of growing up.

It's a long way from fancying someone to going out on a date. It's one thing to be friends with someone. That way, you usually know where you stand. But how do you let someone know that you fancy them, especially if you're worried that they might not fancy you back? The best thing is not to let your nerves get in the way, though it's easier said than done. Try to find something that the person is interested in, then look for a chance to talk to them. Keep it low-key and casual, but don't be afraid to show that you're interested. If the other person doesn't feel the same way – and this happens to everyone – stay cool, accept it and try to move on!

If the other person does feel the same, you might soon find yourself going out on a first date. Don't panic! You could always go out with a group of friends until you feel more comfortable. You should never feel pressured on a date to do anything that you don't want to do. It's normal to want to hold hands, or perhaps have a hug or kiss, but not if you don't feel ready to. Try to listen to your own feelings and do what is right and safe for you.

Ask Dr Christian

I think I might be gay

It's a natural part of growing up to have strong feelings for people. As you grow from being a child, to a teen, to an adult your feelings will develop and change. You will decide that you fancy some people and not others, and some will be of one sex, others may be of another, and all will seem a little confusing. One thing I can say to you is this: none will be wrong. It may take some time for the feelings and urges that you experience to form a pattern until you realize who and what you like.

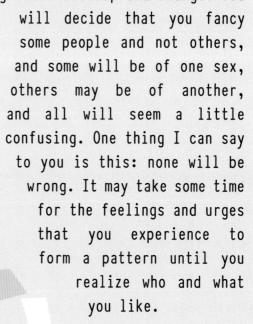

Thinking sexually about both the same sex and the opposite sex is quite common as you grow up. To do so doesn't necessarily mean that you are either gay or straight. Many teens experiment with sexual experiences, including with members of the same sex and these experiences, by themselves, do not necessarily mean that a person is gay or straight either. If you do seem to be mainly attracted to people of your own sex then it can feel like you are the only one, and that everything is designed around straight people, and not for you. You may even hear people talking about gay people in a negative and hurtful way. This may make you want to keep your true feelings secret from others, or pretend to be straight. My advice is to be cautious about who you tell at first but do talk about it to someone. It's not always easy to find somebody to talk to, but many people find that confiding in someone they trust and feel close to, even if they're not completely sure how that person will react, turns out to be a good experience and may help you sort out exactly who and what they like sexually.

STAYING SAFE

Having friends is very important, at any time of your life. But, during puberty, you may find friendships changing as you yourself change, physically and emotionally. You might be best friends with someone one day, then have fallen out spectacularly the next. You might feel that you're being left out when you desperately want to be one of the crowd. These things can make you feel angry or unhappy, but, luckily, they're usually quickly forgotten and you'll find yourselves friends again.

Sometimes, you may feel under pressure to do things just because your friends all seem to be doing them and you don't want to look like the odd one out. This is called peer pressure. Your peers are people who are like you. People give in to peer pressure for various reasons. They might think that they'll lose their friends, or be teased or picked on, if they don't go along with the crowd. They might think that their friends will like them more if they do what they say.

Peer pressure can be positive or negative. You can learn a lot from your peers and get lots of support. But, often peer pressure is negative and leads people into doing things that are bad for them or for other people:

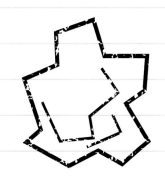

PUTTING OFF YOUR HOMEWORK TO GO OUT

LETTING OTHERS COPY YOUR HOMEWORK

SKIVING OFF SCHOOL OR MISSING SPORTS OR MUSIC CLUBS

SMOKING

DRINKING ALCOHOL

EXPERIMENTING WITH DRUGS

STEALING OR SHOPLIFTING

HAVING SEX BEFORE YOU'RE READY

BULLYING OTHER PEOPLE

Ask Dr Christian

Friendships and peer pressure

Every now and then you will feel pressure from friends to do things that you may not feel happy about, or have been told are not a good idea. This will be a time when your diplomatic skills are required. Someone may offer you alcohol, drugs or a cigarette. Or a boy might suggest that you have sex with him. If you don't feel comfortable will you go ahead anyway or say no and walk away? Sometimes it can be hard. It is easy to feel that doing some of the things your friends are pressuring you to do are necessary to fit in. This is known as peer pressure.

But sometimes peer pressure can be good. Competing with your friends to be better, faster and get better marks than them is all great, and will help you do well.

But if faced with something you are not comfortable with then be strong and say 'no' if it is the right thing to do. Learning to stand up for yourself and your beliefs, and to look ahead to the consequences of your actions, are important steps in becoming a responsible adult.

LOOKING OUT FOR YOURSELF

Everyone has the right to feel safe and secure, and, chances are, that nothing bad is going to happen to you. But part of growing up and becoming an adult is taking more responsibility for yourself and there are lots of things that you can do to help keep yourself safe when you're out and about, or at home. Staying safe online is also very important – you can find out more about this on page 74.

OUT AND ABOUT...

- **IF POSSIBLE, IT'S A GOOD IDEA TO KEEP TOGETHER** with a friend or better still, in a group.

- **STICK TO BUSY, WELL-LIT STREETS**. Don't take short cuts down dark alleyways, even if you're in a hurry.

- **STAY ALERT**. Turn off your MP3 player so that you can hear what's going on around you.

- **NEVER GO OFF WITH A STRANGER** or get into a stranger's car.

- **IF YOU THINK THAT SOMEONE MIGHT BE FOLLOWING YOU,** cross the road or go to somewhere where there are lots of people, such as a shop or bus stop.

- **IF YOU'RE GETTING A BUS OR TRAIN** by yourself, sit with other people if possible.

AT HOME ALONE...

- **IF YOU'RE AT HOME ON YOUR OWN**, keep the front and back doors locked.

- **IF SOMEONE COMES TO THE DOOR**, first check who it is. Don't open the door or let them in unless you know them well.

- **IF THE TELEPHONE RINGS**, don't give out your name and number. If you don't know the caller, don't answer questions about yourself that might give out your personal details.

- **MAKE SURE THAT YOU KNOW** when your parents or carers will be back and where they are.

- **MAKE SURE THAT YOU KNOW** how to phone the emergency services (police, fire, ambulance) and have a list of contact numbers to phone if you need to.

BULLYING

Have you ever been bullied? Bullying is a very big deal. It can be name-calling, teasing, hitting, kicking or stealing – they're all forms of bullying. Bullying can happen to anyone and at any time. You can also be bullied online (see next page). It can make you feel frightened, hurt, or lonely, and it is never okay.

It's hard to feel sorry for bullies but it can help to know why they behave in this way. Often, it's because they're unhappy themselves or are looking for attention. They may think that bullying is big and clever and a way of becoming popular or getting what they want. Bullies often pick on people because it gives them a sense of power to make someone else feel small and miserable. It's the bully that has the problem, not the person that they pick on.

So, if you're being bullied, what can you or should you do? The most important thing is to tell an adult who you can trust. If you're at school, tell a teacher. Your school should also have an anti-bullying policy. You can also tell your parents, or another adult you feel comfortable with. Sometimes, bullies stop as soon as they know that their actions are out in the open. You could also keep a diary of when the bullying takes place and what is said. This will help you to remember everything when you come to speak out. You should also tell someone if you are worried about a friend who might be being bullied.

Remember, no one has the right to bully you or to make you feel bad. Likewise, you do not have the right to bully other people or to make them miserable. Everyone has the right to feel safe and respected.

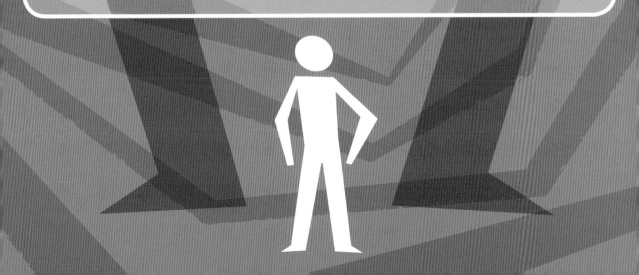

CYBER-BULLYING

Cyber-bullying is when a person or group of people send nasty messages or try to threaten or frighten someone else on the internet or using a mobile phone. It's just as harmful as real-world bullying and it's also against the law. If it happens to you, you need to tell someone immediately. There are different kinds of cyber-bullying. Here are the main ones:

Social networks
Setting up fake profiles to make fun of or bully someone. Posting nasty or threatening comments on people's profiles or on your own status updates.

Internet and email
Sending nasty or threatening emails, or 'hate mails'. This includes sending emails to a group of people to encourage them to take part in the bullying.

Instant messages and chatrooms
Sending nasty or threatening messages and encouraging others to join in the teasing and bullying.

Mobile phones

Sending nasty or threatening texts, phone calls, photos and video messages. Sharing videos showing physical attacks on other people.

Abusing personal information

Pretending to be someone else, without that person's permission. Posting personal photos, emails or blog entries without that person's permission.

If you're being cyber-bullied, it can make you feel very upset and scared, even though it doesn't physically hurt you. It can be difficult to know what to do about it because getting access to the internet or a mobile phone is so easy and messages and information can be sent out so quickly. If it happens to you, don't be tempted to respond to any of the nasty messages or texts. That is just what the bully wants you to do. Instead, keep and save them or write them down, then report them to an adult like a parent or a teacher.

Ask Dr Christian

How do I stay safe online?

You can do all sorts of great things online - chat to friends, listen to music, plan a holiday, buy clothes and watch your favourite movies, all without leaving your own room. But remember - the internet connects you to millions of others across the world, many of whom are strangers who may not be who they say they are. So it is really important to know how to stay safe online and on your mobile.

Never pass on any of your real personal details (such as your address, phone number or school) unless you know the person you're chatting to face-to-face. You don't always know who you're chatting to, and people can easily set up fake profiles and pretend to be someone else.

Keep all of your passwords secret – don't tell anyone else, not even your best friend.

Social networking sites are a great way of keeping in touch but you need to be careful. Think before you add someone as a friend or post information or photos that you wouldn't like your parents or teachers to see. Once you've shared these, you can't take them back and people may use them in ways you don't like.

Don't arrange to meet someone that you only know via the internet. Again, you never quite know who they might be. If you do decide to meet up, take a trusted adult with you, such as a parent, and only meet in a public place.

Keep your mobile phone with you all the time – don't ever lend it to anyone you don't know well. Only give your number to people you know and can trust.

STAYING HEALTHY

While you're growing up, it's very important to stay healthy. This will help you to cope with all the changes, physical and emotional, that are happening to you. Keeping fit and eating a balanced diet will help your body to stay strong and healthy later in life, too.

KEEPING FIT

Exercise is a brilliant way of making your body stronger and healthier. It helps to build up your muscles, strengthen your bones and keep your heart and lungs in good working order. It makes you feel more energetic and is a great way to relax after a hard day at school. It also helps you to stay at a healthy weight. So what's the best kind of exercise to do?

It depends on what you want to do. You can take part in a team sport, or find something you can do on your own. Whatever you do, you don't need to spend loads of money on expensive kit and you can try out different things until you find something that you like. That way, you're more likely to stick at it and, in no time at all, you'll be looking and feeling better.

Here are some sports that you can try:

WALKING
JOGGING
YOGA
SWIMMING
FOOTBALL
DANCING
MARTIAL ARTS
BASKETBALL
CYCLING
TENNIS
SKATEBOARDING
RUGBY
GYMNASTICS
HOCKEY
HORSE-RIDING

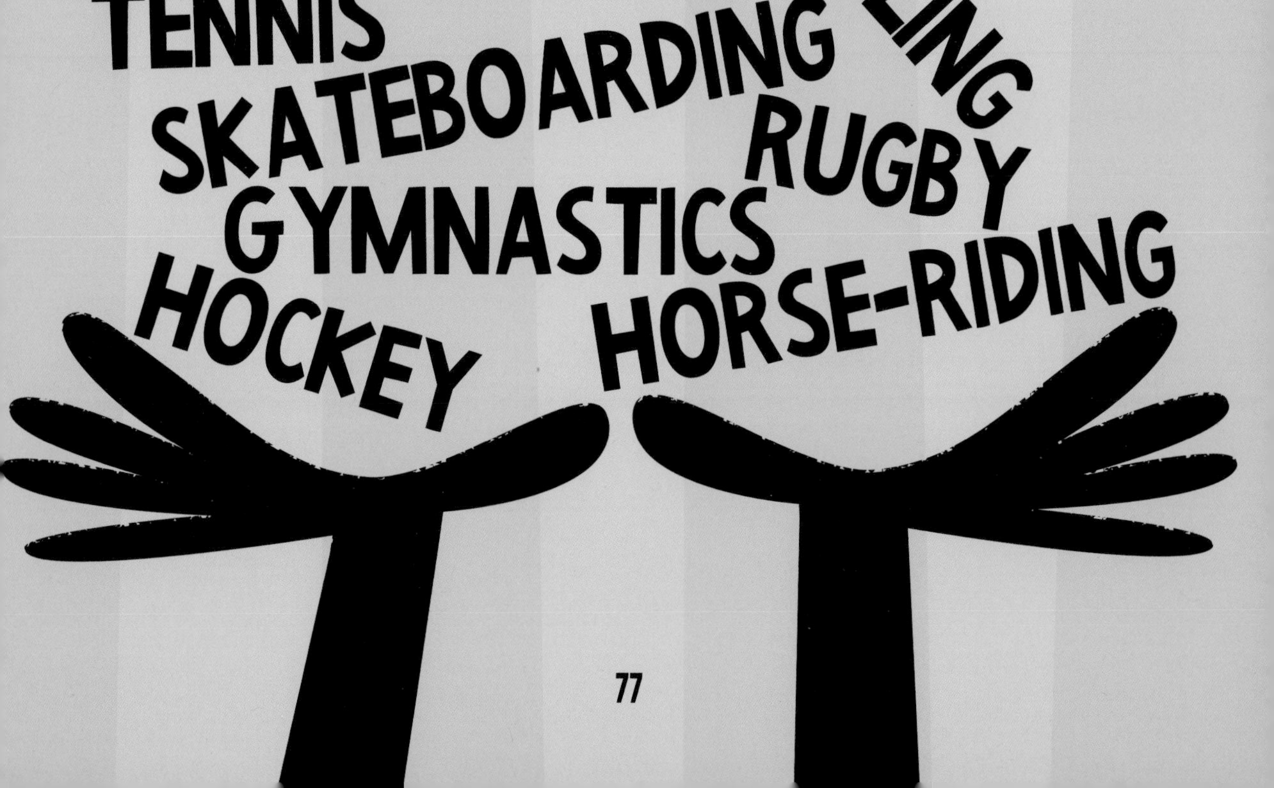

Ask Dr Christian

Exercise mythbusting

If you and your friends are starting to get interested in fitness and exercise, then you will certainly come across all sorts of 'tips' and 'advice' about how to do it best and get the greatest results. A lot of what you hear will be rubbish. Let me set the record straight here.

If your gym teacher says 'no pain, no gain' then you know he or she is talking nonsense. Some occasional muscle aches after exercising is normal, but if anything hurts during sport or exercise then you should stop and get it seen to. Start exercising slowly and build up to avoid injury.

There is no one best way to exercise. Variety is key - so try lots of different stuff out. Most important of all, you should enjoy doing it. And drinking water while you exercise and play sport is very important, and won't hold back your performance.

Try to get the balance right between too little exercise and too much. It only takes about 30 minutes of activity five times a week to make a difference. How do I know how much exercise to do? You are overdoing it if you don't take at least one day off exercise every week, or if your periods start to change or even stop completely.

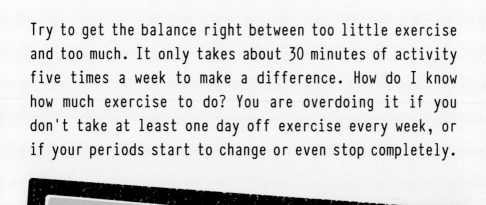

FACT FLASH

Growing up can be exhausting, and it's not just because you're busy keeping fit. We know from plenty of research that teenagers really do need lots of sleep. Otherwise, you'll find yourself getting moodier, more irritable and have trouble concentrating. Also, while you're sleeping, your body releases a hormone that's crucial for your growth and development.

HEALTHY EATING

Because you're growing so fast during puberty, and burning up loads of energy, you'll probably feel hungry a lot of the time. It's easy to be tempted to snack on crisps and chocolate, or skip breakfast to spend an extra half an hour in bed, but it's not a good idea. You need to eat a balanced diet to stay healthy, keep active, and feel and look great.

BALANCED DIET

Eating a variety of different foods will help you to get all the energy and nutrients you need. Have a look at the plate below. It shows you what proportion of each food group you should be eating.

FRUIT AND VEG: eat at least five portions a day, fresh, frozen or tinned. They're packed with essential vitamins and minerals.

BREAD, RICE, POTATOES, PASTA: these are carbs (carbohydrates) and give you energy.

MILK, CHEESE, DAIRY: foods containing calcium for strong bones and teeth.

FATTY AND SUGARY FOODS: food, such as cakes, biscuits, and ice cream that you should only eat in small quantities.

MEAT, FISH, EGGS, BEANS: these provide protein which helps you to grow.

FACT FLASH

SNACK ATTACK
The odd chocolate bar or bag of crisps won't do you any harm but it's better to stick to healthy snacks, such as fruit, nuts or oatcakes. Eat when you're hungry, not just when you're bored, and stop eating when you're full.

WHAT TO DRINK
To stay healthy, your body needs to stay hydrated. Don't wait until you feel thirsty to have a drink. Drink plenty of water – around six glasses a day. It's good for your skin, teeth and body. Steer clear of too many fizzy drinks – they're full of sugar that can rot your teeth.

BODY IMAGE

All the changes that happen to your body during puberty can make you feel self-conscious about how you look. It's completely natural to want to look good – many people have bits of their bodies that they'd like to change – but you also need to be realistic and not to make yourself unhappy by comparing yourself to celebrities and sports stars.

How you see yourself is called your body image, and many people, both boys and girls, have a very negative one. They feel very insecure about how they look and it can have a bad effect on their self-esteem. It doesn't help that the media is full of pictures of beautiful people with seemingly perfect bods, even though these are often fakes.

It's important not to let negative body image affect you so badly that it's all you can think about. If it does, it might help to talk about it to someone. Everyone is different and has a different body type and look. In real-life, very few people look like the celebs you see in magazines. Try not to compare yourself to others – especially the celebs you see in magazines. Everyone is different so focus on the things about you that you like.

EATING DISORDERS

During puberty, it is normal for both boys and girls to put on weight. The trouble starts when people get so worried about their weight that they have serious problems with food and eating which make them ill and unhappy. These are called eating disorders. The two most common types are anorexia nervosa and bulimia.

ANOREXIA NERVOSA: sufferers wrongly see themselves as fat, even when they are very thin, and stop eating to lose weight. They can become very weak and ill, and, without help, some of them can even die.

BULIMIA: sufferers binge (eat lots of food in one go), then make themselves sick so that they don't put on weight. They might also take laxatives. This can cause serious damage to their teeth and bodies.

Ask Dr Christian

Healthy eating/body issues mythbusting

You may notice some girls and boys talking about their weight, comparing themselves to photos in magazines and trying out funny eating habits. Some seem to be really preoccupied and unhappy about their bodies. Not liking your body and the way you look can be very difficult and you must try to talk to someone about it.

Controlling your food so that you are often hungry is never good and will lead to all sorts of problems when you are older. Food is to be enjoyed and is usually a big part of going out with friends and at parties.

I can assure you that funny celebrity diets do not work and can cause your weight to yo-yo up and down uncontrollably.

Always remember that what you look like is NOT more important than what you do. You can do or be anything you want to be, it's down to hard work and dedication, and not how tall you are or what colour your hair is.

If your friends do seem to have funny issues with food you should know that it is often not really because they don't like food, but because they are not happy with themselves inside and you should try to encourage them to talk to someone about it.

If looking at amazing pictures of beautiful models in magazines makes you feel bad about yourself then let me tell you a little secret. They don't really look like that! Have a look at my photo on the front cover of this book. What do you think? Not bad, eh? But I had someone to choose my clothes, someone to do my hair, someone to put on some make-up (yes, make-up!) to even out my skin and make me look fresher, and after the pictures were taken, someone took out all the imperfections using a computer, before this cover photo was chosen and printed. You should see me first thing in the morning - I frighten myself looking in the mirror!

PERSONAL HYGIENE

You'll need to start taking extra care of your personal hygiene, and wash more often as you get older. This is because, during puberty, you start to sweat more. You have sweat glands all over your body, and sweat is very useful for cooling your body down on a hot day or when you're doing exercise. But, during puberty, you start to sweat differently, especially around your armpits and groin. And, if the sweat mixes with bacteria on your skin, it can make you smelly. The smell's called body odour, or BO, for short.

To make sure that you don't get BO, have a bath or shower every day. Wash your armpits and genitals thoroughly with mild soap. Hang your towel up after you've used it and change it every few days. (Wash your feet every day, too. They're also covered in sweat glands and get very stinky after they've been crammed in socks and shoes all day.) It's also important to change your clothes every day, and especially before they get whiffy.

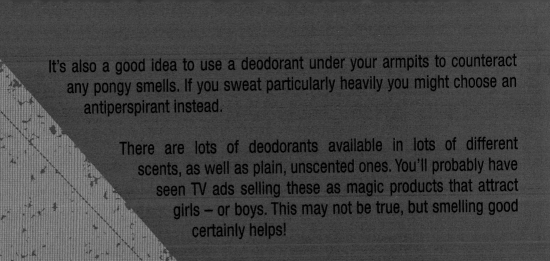

It's also a good idea to use a deodorant under your armpits to counteract any pongy smells. If you sweat particularly heavily you might choose an antiperspirant instead.

There are lots of deodorants available in lots of different scents, as well as plain, unscented ones. You'll probably have seen TV ads selling these as magic products that attract girls – or boys. This may not be true, but smelling good certainly helps!

OILY HAIR

During puberty, oil-producing sebaceous glands go into overdrive! Too much oil, or sebum, can make your hair look greasy, so if you have this problem it's a good idea to wash your every day using a shampoo that's formulated for oily hair.

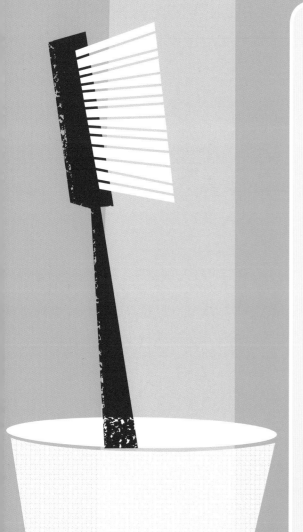

HEALTHY TEETH

By the time you're about 14, you will probably have most of your adult teeth. They need to last you for life so you should take really good care of them. Brush them with a fluoride toothpaste twice a day – after breakfast and before you go to bed – for at least two minutes at a time. Clean your teeth with floss before bedtime to get rid of any hidden specks of food. Change your toothbrush regularly – bacteria is quick to build up on the bristles.

If your adult teeth grow crooked, you might need to wear braces to straighten them out. Braces are nothing to worry about but they do take a bit of getting used to. Your orthodontist will fit them and tell you how to look after them. The most important thing is to keep them clean and not let food get stuck in them, otherwise it will rot your teeth. And, remember, it'll be worth it in the end.

LOOK
AFTER
YOUR
EYES

Your eyes and eyesight are really precious so looking after them makes sense. A healthy diet and exercise can help, as can getting enough sleep. Don't spend too long staring at TV or computer screens – the glare can strain your eyes. It's also a good idea to have regular eye tests so that an optician can check that everything is okay. And if you do need glasses, make sure that you wear them so that your eyes don't get sore and tired. When you're older, you might try wearing contact lenses but you'll need to ask your optician for advice.

AND THAT'S IT...

I hope you found this book useful and that it has helped prepare you for some of the things that are to come, or explained some of the things that are happening to you right now. Hopefully both. Growing up isn't easy. Some parts you will hate, others you will love, and many you will find confusing. But we all have to go through it, so you know you can always talk to someone, and always ask questions if you need to. No one will think you are silly for doing so. Spend some time by yourself thinking things through; about who and what you are, and who and what you want to be. It's going to be fun, I promise.

Good luck!

Dr Christian

GLOSSARY

ACNE Red, inflamed spots on the face, chest, back or shoulders that often appear during puberty.

CONTRACEPTION Devices or drugs, such as condoms or the Pill, used to prevent a pregnancy.

EATING DISORDERS Illnesses, such as anorexia or bulimia, caused when people have a problem with food and eating.

EGG A female sex cell. produced in a woman's ovaries. If an egg joins with a male's sperm, a baby may start growing.

ERECTION When a man gets sexually excited and his penis grow stiff as more blood flows into it.

FERTILIZES When a male sperm joins with a female egg so that a baby can grow.

GENES Codes or instructions in your cells that are passed down to you by your parents. They control your height, hair and eye colour, and other body features.

GENITALS The sex organs on the outside of the body.

HORMONES Powerful chemicals that travel around your body in your blood. They include sex hormones. They send messages to different parts of your body, affecting what they do.

MASTURBATING Touching or rubbing your sex organs for pleasure.

MENSTRUAL CYCLE The number of days from the beginning of one period to another – usually about 28 days.

OESTROGEN A female sex hormone.

ORGASM In males the muscular contractions that lead to the expulsion of sperm from the penis. In females pleasurable contractions of the muscles in the vagina and uterus.

OVARIES A woman's sex organs. They produce female sex hormones and eggs. Women have two ovaries in the lower abdomen, on either side of the uterus.

PENIS A male's external sex organ.

PERIODS The monthly bleed that women have when unfertilized eggs and the uterus lining are released from their bodies.

PREGNANT When a baby starts growing from a fertilized egg inside a woman's uterus. Pregnancy usually lasts for about 40 weeks.

PROGESTERONE A female sex hormone.

PUBIC HAIR Short, wiry hair that grows around your external sex organs during puberty.

SEX ORGANS The parts of the body necessary for reproduction (making babies).

SPERM A male sex cell, produced in a man's testicles. A sperm joins with a female's egg to make a baby.

TESTOSTERONE A male sex hormone.

TOXIC SHOCK SYNDROME A rare but life-threatening bacterial infection that occurs when certain bacteria which normally live harmlessly on the skin invade the body's bloodstream and release poisonous toxins, causing sudden high fever and a massive drop in blood pressure.

VAGINA A stretchy, muscular tube that leads from a woman's uterus to the outside of her body.

OTHER RESOURCES

UK WEBSITES

http://www.childline.org.uk/explore/Pages/Explore.aspx

Advice - presented by Radio 1, 1Xtra and BBC Switch gives you the straight facts on teen issues from sexual health and bullying to drink and drugs.

http://www.bbc.co.uk/radio1/advice/your_body/boys_bodies
http://www.bbc.co.uk/radio1/advice/your_body/girls_bodies

www.likeitis.org
www.childrenfirst.nhs.uk/teens/life/puberty_body_tour/index.html

US WEBSITES

http://kidshealth.org/
http://puberty101.com/
http://www.girlshealth.gov/body/puberty/index.html